YOUR CHOICE, SNOOPY

by Charles M. Schulz

Selected Cartoons from
You're Something Else, Charlie Brown, Vol. 1

FAWCETT CREST • NEW YORK

YOUR CHOICE, SNOOPY

This book, prepared especially for Fawcett Crest Books, a unit of CBS Publications, the Consumer Publishing Division of CBS Inc., comprises the first half of YOU'RE SOMETHING ELSE, CHARLIE BROWN, and is reprinted by arrangement with Holt, Rinehart & Winston, Inc.

ISBN: 0-449-23882-2

Printed in the United States of America

First Fawcett Crest Printing: November 1973

23   22   21   20   19   18   17   16   15   14

Your Choice, Snoopy!

flitter
flitter
flitter

I CAN'T FIGURE THAT GUY OUT...

HE'S EITHER A LOUSY FLYER OR HIS BLOOD SUGAR'S DOWN

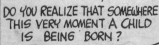

HAVE YOU BEEN USING MY CRAYONS?

WHY, YES... I BORROWED THEM YESTERDAY TO DRAW SOME PICTURES....

WELL, WHAT HAPPENED TO THE BLUE? THE BLUE IS GONE!

I DREW A LOT OF SKIES!

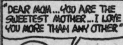

BONK!

I'LL NEVER BE A GOOD MANAGER....
I HATE TO AWAKEN AN INFIELDER
WHO'S SLEEPING SO PEACEFULLY!

"'ALL RIGHT,' SAID THE CAT; AND THIS TIME IT VANISHED QUITE SLOWLY...

BEGINNING WITH THE END OF THE TAIL, AND ENDING WITH THE GRIN, WHICH REMAINED SOME TIME AFTER THE REST OF IT HAD GONE."

I'VE BEEN ABLE TO DO THAT FOR YEARS!

IF YOU PULL ANY OF THAT CHESHIRE-BEAGLE STUFF ON ME I'LL POUND YOU!!

RATS!

DEAR PEN PAL,
TODAY I TAKE PEN
IN HAND.

I AM VERY PROUD
OF MYSELF.

SO FAR I HAVEN'T
SMEARED A SINGLE

WO~~RD~~

SCHULZ

➡

RIGHT IN THE MIDDLE OF A BALL GAME?

ARE YOU OUT OF YOUR MIND?!

I'M TRYING TO PITCH, CAN'T YOU SEE THAT?!! I'VE GOT TO CONCENTRATE ON WHAT I'M DOING!

OH, NOW YOU'RE GOING TO BE HURT, AREN'T YOU? OH, GOOD GRIEF, ALL RIGHT... COME HERE...

SKRITCH
SKRITCH
SKRITCH
SKRITCH
SKRITCH

SIGH!

NO WONDER SANDY KOUFAX RETIRED!

NINE HOME RUNS IN A ROW!! GOOD GRIEF!

WHAT CAN I DO?!!

WE'RE GETTING SLAUGHTERED AGAIN, SCHROEDER... I DON'T KNOW WHAT TO DO...WHY DO WE HAVE TO SUFFER LIKE THIS?

"MAN IS BORN TO TROUBLE AS THE SPARKS FLY UPWARD."

WHAT?

HE'S QUOTING FROM THE "BOOK OF JOB", CHARLIE BROWN... SEVENTH VERSE, FIFTH CHAPTER....

CHUCK, I'D LIKE TO HAVE YOU MEET JOSÉ PETERSON..

NOW, THE WAY I SEE IT, CHUCK, YOU CAN PLAY JOSÉ PETERSON HERE AT SECOND WHERE HE CAN WORK WITH THAT FUNNY-LOOKING KID YOU'VE GOT PLAYING SHORTSTOP...

WHAT ABOUT LINUS? HE'S ALWAYS PLAYED A PRETTY GOOD SECOND BASE...

DON'T WORRY ABOUT LINUS... I'LL EXPLAIN THE WHOLE THING TO HIM..

HI, SWEETIE!

THAT'S THE WAY JOSÉ PETERSON HIT THE YEAR HIS FAMILY LIVED IN NEW MEXICO...

THAT'S THE WAY JOSÉ PETERSON HIT THE YEAR HIS FAMILY LIVED IN NORTH DAKOTA...

NOW LOOK, CHUCK... HERE'S THE WAY YOUR NEW LINEUP CAN GO...

WITH JOSÉ PETERSON AT SECOND AND ME TAKING OVER THE MOUND CHORES, YOU'RE GOING TO HAVE A GREAT TEAM, YES, SIR!

NOBODY WILL BE ABLE TO BEAT US! WHY, YOU'LL PROBABLY BE SELECTED "MANAGER OF THE YEAR"!

FOR WHAT?

PAT
PAT
PAT
PAT
PAT

※ SIGH ※

I THINK I'VE FOUND
MY CALLING!

YOUR BROTHER PATS BIRDS ON THE HEAD!

THAT'S A **TERRIBLE** THING TO SAY TO SOMEONE THE FIRST THING IN THE MORNING!

PAT
PAT
PAT
PAT

THEY COME DEPRESSED, AND THEY GO AWAY FEELING GREAT

SORRY, BIRD..

SCHULZ

BOOT!

"THIS IS 'BE KIND TO ANIMALS WEEK'"

WELL, SNOOPY, HERE WE ARE AT SUMMER CAMP...

THE FIRST THING THEY'LL DO IS ASSIGN US TO A BARRACKS, AND THEN WE'LL HAVE LUNCH...

NOT "LUNCH"... CHOW! WE WORLD WAR I FLYING ACES ALWAYS CALL IT "CHOW"... WHAT A MISERABLE CAMP. WE MUST BE FIFTY KILOMETERS FROM THE NEAREST VILLAGE! CURSE THIS HOT WEATHER! CURSE THIS STUPID WAR!

WE WORLD WAR I FLYING ACES DO A LOT OF GRIPING!

HERE'S THE WORLD WAR I FLYING ACE STANDING OUT UNDER THE STARS...IT'S A BEAUTIFUL NIGHT...

SOMEWHERE OFF IN THE DISTANCE IS THE LOW RUMBLE OF ARTILLERY FIRE.. AS HE LOOKS AT THE SKY, HE THINKS OF THE PEOPLE AT HOME, AND WONDERS IF THEY'RE LOOKING AT THE SAME SKY...AND THEN HE IS SAD...

SLOWLY HE WALKS BACK ACROSS THE DARKENED AERODROME, AND THEN THE THOUGHT THAT THROBS SO CONSTANTLY IN HIS MIND CRIES OUT..

CURSE YOU, RED BARON!

SCHULZ

HEY, CHARLIE BROWN, COME QUICK! THEY'RE HAVING A CANOE RACE!

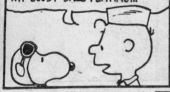

A CANOE RACE?! C'MON, SNOOPY...IF WE CAN WIN THE CANOE RACE, EVERYONE WILL FORGET ABOUT MY LOUSY BALL PLAYING...

WE'LL SHOW 'EM, SNOOPY...WE'LL GET IN THIS CANOE, WE'LL WIN THIS RACE AND WE'LL BE HEROES!

ACTUALLY, I HAD PLANNED FOR YOU TO HELP WITH THE PADDLING..

ACTUALLY, A SMILE MAKES A LOUSY UMBRELLA!

I DON'T UNDERSTAND YOU... WHY DO YOU HAVE TO PLAY SHORTSTOP WITH YOUR SUPPER DISH IN YOUR MOUTH?

BECAUSE I DON'T HAVE A POCKET!

I SUPPOSE I COULD LIE HERE IN THE DARK FOR THE REST OF MY LIFE...

IT'S KIND OF NICE TO BE ABLE TO WITHDRAW FROM ALL YOUR PROBLEMS. IT'S NICE TO BE ABLE TO FORGET YOUR RESPONSIBILITIES, AND....

RESPONSIBILITIES?!! GOOD GRIEF, I FORGOT TO FEED MY DOG!

VERY PECULIAR LOOKING WAITER...PROBABLY SOME POOR BLIGHTER JUST OUT OF THE TRENCHES!

JUST TO SHOW YOU THAT I'M NOT SELFISH, I'LL SHARE IT WITH YOU... HOLD OUT YOUR HANDS...

!

SLURP!

SLURP!

SLURP!

LOOK, LINUS, I GOT MY KITE IN THE AIR! CONGRATULATE ME!

CONGRATULATIONS, CHARLIE BROWN!

YOU **BLOCKHEAD**! I'LL BET YOU TOUCHED ALMOST EVERY LEMON DROP IN THIS BAG! YOU ONLY TOOK ONE...WHY DID YOU HAVE TO RATTLE YOUR FINGERS AROUND? DO YOU EXPECT ME TO EAT A BUNCH OF LEMON DROPS YOU'VE **TOUCHED**?!

HERE! YOU TAKE EVERY LEMON DROP OUT OF THERE THAT YOU TOUCHED! I'M NOT GOING TO EAT CANDY YOU'VE TOUCHED WITH YOUR FINGERS!

WELL, THIS ONE LOOKS LIKE I MAY HAVE TOUCHED IT, AND THIS ONE, TOO, AND MAYBE THIS ONE, AND PERHAPS THIS ONE, AND...

CARE FOR A LEMON DROP?

POW!

JUST WHAT I'VE ALWAYS WANTED...A ROOMFUL OF LEMON DROPS!

MORE PEANUTS®

JOGGING IS IN, SNOOPY
   (selected cartoons from
   The Beagle Has Landed, Vol. 1)   24344 $1.5

STAY WITH IT, SNOOPY!
   (selected cartoons from
   Summers Walk, Winters Fly, Vol. 3)   24310 $1.5

YOU'RE A PAL, SNOOPY!
   (selected cartoons from
   You Need Help, Charlie Brown, Vol. 2)   23775 $1.2

PLAY BALL, SNOOPY
   (selected cartoons from
   Win a Few, Lose a Few, Charlie Brown, Vol. 1) 23222 $1.50

YOU'VE GOT TO BE KIDDING, SNOOPY!
   (selected cartoons from
   Speak Softly and Carry a Beagle, Vol. 1)   23453 $1.25

HERE'S TO YOU, CHARLIE BROWN.
   (selected cartoons from
   You Can't Win, Charlie Brown, Vol. 2)   23708 $1.50

Buy them at your local bookstore or use this handy coupon for ordering.

COLUMBIA BOOK SERVICE (a CBS Publications Co.)
32275 Mally Road, P.O. Box FB, Madison Heights, MI 48071

Please send me the books I have checked above. Orders for less than 5 books
must include 75¢ for the first book and 25¢ for each additional book to cover
postage and handling. Orders for 5 books or more postage is FREE. Send
check or money order only.

    Cost $_____   Name_____

Sales tax*_____   Address_____

  Postage_____   City_____

   Total $_____   State_____Zip_____
**The government requires us to collect sales tax in all states except AK,
DE, MT, NH and OR.*

This offer expires 1 November 81   8135